Boise State University Western Writers Series   Number 51

Horace McCoy

By Mark Royden Winchell
University of Southern Mississippi

Editors: Wayne Chatterton
James H. Maguire

Business Manager:
James Hadden

Cover Design and Illustration
by Arny Skov, Copyright 1982

Boise State University, Boise, Idaho

Copyright 1982
by the
Boise State University Western Writers Series

ALL RIGHTS RESERVED

Library of Congress Card No. 82-71031

International Standard Book No. 0-88430-025-0

Printed in the United States of America by
J & D Printing
Meridian, Idaho

Horace McCoy

Horace McCoy

Upon returning from Paris in 1946, *Vogue* editor Allene Talmey observed: "Everyone in the knowledgeable world talks about American writers, about a curious trinity: Hemingway, Faulkner, and McCoy" ("Paris Quick Notes/About Sartre, Gide, Cocteau, Politics,/The Theatre, and Inflation," *Vogue*, January 15, 1947, p. 92). Although he has long had an enthusiastic following overseas, the California novelist Horace McCoy (1897-1955) is virtually unknown in the United States. Here, all five of his novels are out of print and the published scholarship on those novels is minimal. Nevertheless, McCoy was a serious artist who helped extend the boundaries of the indigenously American genre of hard-boiled or tough-guy fiction. Moreover, his life and work demonstrate the paradoxical significance of the West within our national mythology.

The eldest of five children, Horace Stanley McCoy was born on April 14, 1897, in a cabin near Pegram Station, Tennessee. His mother—Nannie Holt McCoy—was an impoverished but well-educated descendant of the Southern aristocracy, and his father—James Harris McCoy—a former schoolteacher who had become a conductor on the Nashville, Chatanooga, and Saint Louis Railroad. When Horace was two, James McCoy moved his family twenty miles east to Nashville.

Although he spent the first eighteen years of his life in middle Tennessee, McCoy did not use this region or the experiences of his childhood as a source for his later fiction. Indeed, he is one of the least Southern of modern American novelists. Nor does Tennessee seem eager to claim him as a native son. The only one of his books available in the Nashville area is a Portuguese translation of *They Shoot Horses, Don't They?* at the Vanderbilt University Library.

By 1913, McCoy had dropped out of high school and was working as an auto mechanic and travelling salesman. Then, in 1915, the family moved to Dallas. It was here that McCoy would spend his young adulthood and develop the artistic ambitions which would remain with him for the rest of his life. His most crucial experiences in Dallas, however, were still before him when — in 1917 — he went off to World War I.

Of the same generation as Hemingway and the poets of Georgian England, McCoy nevertheless responded much differently than they to "the war to end all wars." No political idealist, he enlisted in the air corps in a spirit of pure adventure. He had no painful lessons to learn, no separate peace to make. Although he was hit by machine-gun fire, he suffered no very serious wound. Judging from his letters home, it seems that McCoy was primarily concerned with advancement in military rank. Whereas other future writers viewed the war with anguished introspection, McCoy was detached from its more profound horrors. If his wartime experience had any literary impact at all, it was in enabling him to perceive violence with the cool objectivity characteristic of the hard-boiled school.

During his final weeks in Europe, McCoy served as public relations man for an entertainment revue and — in the process — became convinced that he possessed latent journalistic talents. Thus, upon returning home, he represented himself to the *Dallas Morning News* as a veteran of the *New York Tribune.* Two days into this new job, he was fired as an obvious imposter.

After resorting to menial labor for a while, McCoy subsequently was hired by the sensation-mongering *Dallas Dispatch.* Here, he was a regular columnist for both the sports and amusement pages, as well as a legendary general-news reporter. In fact, his news stories were so impressive that Harry Clay Withers, managing editor of the *Dallas Journal*, hired him away from the *Dispatch*, only to discover that his new reporter's earlier scoops were largely fiction. Although he may have lacked a sense of professional ethics, McCoy clearly possessed a fertile imagination.

Despite his success in newspaper work, McCoy was not confined to expressing himself exclusively through the *written* word. A noted actor in the highly acclaimed Dallas Little Theatre, he originally intended to gain fame in Hollywood in front of a camera rather than behind a typewriter. Between 1925 and 1931, McCoy appeared in ten productions of the Dallas Little Theatre—his most memorable performances being as Geert in Herman Heijermans' *The Good Hope*, as Joe in Sidney Howard's *They Knew What They Wanted*, and as the title character in Ferenc Molnár's *Liliom*.

What appeared to be McCoy's big break came when an MGM scout saw him in a Little Theatre production and held out the possibility of a screentest. At the same time, that scout signed the real object of his quest—McCoy's director Oliver Hinsdell—to an immediate contract. So, in the spring of 1931, director and protégé left for Hollywood. All that McCoy had was the promise of Hinsdell's help, a free ride to California, and a consuming ambition which could no longer be satisfied within the provincial confines of Dallas.

While still a Texas journalist, McCoy began his career as a serious fiction writer by selling stories to the tabloid *Black Mask*. Founded by H. L. Mencken and George Jean Nathan in 1920, *Black Mask* would become the primary vehicle for hard-boiled fiction in the second quarter of the twentieth century. The writers who appeared regularly in its pages included Carroll John Daly, Raoul Whitfield, Erle Stanley Gardner, James M. Cain, Raymond Chandler, and Dashiell

Hammett. Among other achievements, this publication was responsible for creating the prototype of the modern private detective—so different in lifestyle and sensibility from the creations of Edgar Allan Poe and Arthur Conan Doyle.

The man who gave *Black Mask* its identity, and who provided Horace McCoy with his first national audience, was the magazine's avuncular editor Joseph T. Shaw. Proscribing discursive commentary and abstract language, Shaw insisted that the stories in *Black Mask* reveal internal conflicts through external action, that they *show* rather than *tell*. One of the results of this terse objectivity, according to Ernest Borneman, was that *Black Mask* "contributed to the development of what Mencken called 'the American language'—a prose style which, by transcending the limits of the crime story, has become part and parcel of the serious American novel" ("Black Mask," *Go*, February-March, 1952, p. 63).

Of the sixteen stories which McCoy published in *Black Mask* between September 1929 and October 1934, all but two deal with the exploits of an airborne Texas Ranger named Jerry Frost. As J. Thomas Sturak has noted, Frost is a cross between the "romantic paragons of popular Western fiction and the mechanical supermen of air-war stories" ("The Life and Writings of Horace McCoy, 1897-1955," Diss. UCLA 1967, p. 205). Because McCoy's interest in social and psychological issues causes him occasionally to digress from the main narrative line, these stories ultimately fall short of the *Black Mask* ideal of "pure" action. Even in this early, formulaic fiction, he was striving—however unsuccessfully—to express a larger vision of the world.

Although he did appear in a few minor movie roles, it became apparent by the mid-thirties that Horace McCoy would have to make his living as a writer, not as an actor. His experience as a frustrated film extra, however, was not wasted; for it provided the raw material for two of his novels—*They Shoot Horses, Don't They?* and *I Should Have Stayed Home.*

They Shoot Horses (1935) had the misfortune to appear at the height of the Depression, when the reading tastes of an economically beleagured nation ran to escapist fiction. In addition, because of some superficial resemblances between McCoy's novel and James M. Cain's *The Postman Always Rings Twice* (1934), critics from Edmund Wilson to Walter Winchell dismissed the more recent of the two works as derivative. Sturak, however, points out that a short-story version of *They Shoot Horses* was on paper two years prior to the publication of *Postman*; and that the first draft of McCoy's book-length manuscript was completed by late 1933.

As the basis for his next novel, *No Pockets in a Shroud* (1937), McCoy turned to his early life as a newspaperman and amateur actor in Dallas. Although fast-paced and topical, this highly idealized bit of autobiographical fiction could not find an American publisher. It was brought out in England by Arthur Barker, but has never appeared in its original form in the United States.

Except for a couple of short stories, McCoy produced no fiction for ten years after his third novel—*I Should Have Stayed Home*—was published in 1938. During this time, he was making a living as a scriptwriter on B pictures, apparently resigned to the fate of a hack. What he did not know was that even then his reputation was growing in Europe, particularly in England, Scandinavia, and France. Indeed, in 1944 a translation of *They Shoot Horses, Don't They?* was printed and distributed by the French Resistance movement.

At the point of vocational despondency, McCoy saw Allene Talmey's mention of him in *Vogue*. The popularity of his novels among European intellectuals, especially French existentialists, prodded him to return to serious fiction. In 1948, he made his fourth novel—*Kiss Tomorrow Good-bye*—a crucial test of his literary talent. This psychological gangster tale was meant to liberate him from Hollywood and to establish his claim as a major writer. Instead, it became a critically-panned best-seller and the only one of his novels to be filmed during McCoy's lifetime.

In 1951, Horace McCoy returned to France for the first time since World War I. There he met a number of leading literary figures, including Jean Paul Sartre. In failing health and with only a few more years to live, McCoy would never fully realize his desire for critical acclaim. A commercial success and an artistic failure, his fifth novel *Scalpel* (1952) was also his last.

At the time of his death, McCoy was forty-six pages into what would have been his sixth novel. Overweight and prematurely aged, he bore little resemblance to the dashing actor of his youth. "On Thursday night, December 15, 1955," writes Sturak, "he sat down in the living-room of his home, having just turned on the television set. His wife, in another room, heard him call out to her. By the time she reached him he was slumped in his chair, dead of a heart attack" (p. 543).

A good place to begin a discussion of McCoy's fiction would be *No Pockets in a Shroud*, its author's most autobiographical novel. Completed by the end of March 1936, this book made the rounds of American publishers in the summer and fall of that year. Despite their appreciation of McCoy's narrative powers, none of these publishers found his work to be sufficiently convincing or coherent. It was not until 1948 that a considerably revised version of *No Pockets in a Shroud* appeared in paperback as the "first U.S. edition." By that time, the original had been published in London, Copenhagen, Paris, and Stockholm.

The novel's setting is Colton, a town very much like Dallas of the 1920s. McCoy's protagonist—Michael Dolan—is a headstrong, sexually irresistible newspaper reporter and Little Theatre actor. The story begins when Dolan resigns in anger from the Colton *Daily Times-Gazette* after having been chastised for his exposure of a local baseball scandal and for his continuing debts to some of the paper's more substantial advertisers. Undaunted, Dolan secures a loan from a wealthy Little Theatre colleague to begin a rather hybrid city magazine — *The Cosmopolite* — combining high-society features with investigative reporting.

At the same time, Dolan's homelife — a quasi-Bohemian existence which he shares with six roommates in a dilapidated three-story house — is complicated by his attempts alternately to satisfy and fend off a seemingly endless stream of women, who come in all ages and from every stratum of society. The one who finally wins Dolan's hand (if not his heart or exclusive claim on his body) is Myra Barnovsky, a New York Communist who shows up in Colton on the day that Dolan leaves the *Times-Gazette* and who becomes his girl-Friday on the *Cosmopolite*.

Michael's private amours and public muckraking complement each other as McCoy's protagonist keeps his magazine afloat by borrowing money from a well-heeled matron whose bed he occasionally shares and by extorting a large settlement for agreeing to the annulment of his sudden marriage to a politician's daughter. Despite attempted bribery (by local newspapers) and physical intimidation (by one of the town's most powerful and corrupt citizens), Dolan continues to publish his magazine.

The novel's denouement occurs when Dolan manages to infiltrate a gathering of the Crusaders, a vigilante group modelled on the Ku Klux Klan. Concealed behind a pilfered robe and hood, he witnesses the tar-and-feathering of an old black agitator and the castration of a young white rake. He also copies down the license-plate numbers of others in attendance — a group which includes some of Colton's most prominent townspeople. Upon publishing an exposé in the

Cosmopolite, Dolan prepares to testify before a Grand Jury investigating the Crusaders. Before he can do so, however, he is murdered in an alley near his office.

To call *No Pockets in a Shroud* an autobiographical novel is not to suggest that it provides reliable information about its author's life in Dallas. The superficial similarities between McCoy and Dolan prove only that McCoy, like so many of the rest of us, was able to create a Walter Mitty image of himself. Like his protagonist, the author was a Little Theatre actor and journalist who briefly edited a city magazine, a *New Yorker manqué—The Dallasite*—which occasionally printed stories the more conservative daily papers considered too hot to handle; and, like Dolan, McCoy did live for a time in a quasi-Bohemian commune. But the novel's more melodramatic moments are pure fiction and its eroticism largely soft-core fantasy.

McCoy's second novel is "autobiographical" not because of its factual authenticity, but because of what it reveals about certain conflicts within its author's psyche. For one thing, McCoy—like F. Scott Fitzgerald—had strongly ambivalent feelings about the rich. The protagonist of each of his novels is an outsider who dreams of social success and who finds the promise of that success to lie in the patronage of one or more wealthy women.

Similarly, McCoy was himself married to two women who had more money and social prominence than he. Although he may have had some misgivings about a seeming inability to "make it" on his own, he nevertheless valued the advantages of marrying above his station. By the same token, Dolan says of Colton's country-club set: "in spite of everything, they represent something I've never had and something I want very much" (p. 77).

No doubt, much of this novel's European popularity during the late 1930s and early forties was due to its political overtones. At one level, McCoy is attacking domestic fascism, press timidity, and the ruthless venality of America's ruling class. Nor was he reluctant to draw explicit analogies between local and global tyranny. Thinking about Colton's own despot, Michael reflects: "there was a Carlisle in every town in the country, but . . . millions upon millions were too stupid to care, and . . . it was that way all over the world: millions upon millions of people who believed Hitler and Mussolini were great fellows" (p. 154).

Of course, the theme of social protest has had a venerable tradition in American literature. The two best-selling American novels in the nineteenth century—Harriet Beecher Stowe's *Uncle Tom's Cabin* (1852) and Edward Bellamy's *Looking Backward* (1888)—were both political tracts in the form of fiction. Never was the social consciousness of U.S. writers more agitated, however, than during the Depression-era thirties. Like his friend Nathanael West, McCoy was sympathetic to the left-wing influences operating in Hollywood. Accordingly, *No Pockets in a Shroud* depicts a virtuous Left and a demonic Right. Two of Dolan's closest associates on the *Cosmopolite* are card-carrying Communists, while the vigilante Crusaders are "America First" advocates who give the Hitler salute.

And yet, judged solely as a political novel, *No Pockets* is less than totally successful. For one thing, Mike Dolan seems to be motivated less by idealism than by spite. Such an orientation might be effective were he a revolutionary seeking to destroy an evil system of government. Instead, he all too often resembles what Myra accuses him of being—"a frustrated cotillion leader." The divided nature of his magazine mirrors Dolan's own envious resentment of the trappings of aristocracy.

Because Michael is so preoccupied with a personal agenda, he appears to lack a sense of moral priorities. The evils of a baseball fix and of arbitrary politics in the Little Theatre seem to enrage him almost as much as do the butchery of a back-alley abortionist and the brutality of the Crusaders. Since McCoy fails to introduce any irony into his characterization of Dolan, we must conclude that the author himself makes little distinction between mortal and venial injustices.

The ideology informing this novel is one of class struggle. As a result, McCoy avoids dealing with any sociological nuances which might complicate his rigid schematics. Thus, the Crusaders consist largely of the town gentry, when—in reality—such groups generally tend to be formed among the lower and lower-middle classes. (Upper-class bigots are able to work their will in more subtle if no less violent ways.)

Also, from the standpoint of the 1980s, McCoy's depiction of blacks is grotesquely dated. The novel's most embarrassingly stereotypical character is an obsequious young darky named Ulysses who serves as a kind of butler, valet, and all-around doormat for Dolan and his roommates. Even though the boys have long since stopped paying him his $20-a-month salary, he remains attentive to their every need and accepts their verbal abuse with a simple-minded equanimity. Apparently, "Mr. Mike's" vision of a new social order is far from color-blind.

As one might expect, McCoy's women hardly fare better. It may be necessary, in terms of the dialectic of class struggle, to portray the Colton debutantes as vapid nymphomaniacs; but one might at least expect the Communist Myra Barnovsky to be a contrasting symbol of working-class idealism and integrity. Instead, Myrna seems to be more interested in gaining precedence in Dolan's bed than in establishing the dictatorship of the proletariat.

Perhaps the most fruitful way of approaching *No Pockets in a Shroud* would be to look beyond its politics and to view the novel as a tale of hard-boiled individualism. When Michael's friend Eddie Bishop tries to convince McCoy's protagonist that the only hope for achieving permanent social reform lies in submitting oneself to the regimentation of the Communist Party, Dolan replies: "Maybe I am a Communist. If I am, I don't know it. But I do hate all the things you say I hate, and a lot more you didn't mention. . . . Maybe I do need discipline and organization, and maybe later on I'll get somebody to teach them to me. But I haven't got time to stop for that now" (pp. 232-33).

If we look at Michael as a *Black Mask* hero who has been thrust into a political context, then his characterization begins to make a bit of sense. He is the resourceful *individual*, trying to survive in a hostile environment. Even if his struggle is ultimately doomed, it is his tenacity in that struggle and his refusal to take refuge in systems or ideologies that make Dolan the sort of figure with whom existentialists could identify. As John Killinger notes: *"The basic attempt of all existentialism has been to establish the separate identity of the individual" (Hemingway and the Dead Gods,* p. 6).

The title of McCoy's novel also stresses one of the central tenets of existentialism—the primacy of the here-and-now. What meaning there is in life can never be determined *a priori,* nor can it be validated eschatologically. When Bishop points out to Dolan the unlikelihood of his getting rich from investigative journalism, Michael replies: "Well, they're no pockets in a shroud" (p. 233). This statement is simply a more lurid version of the aphorism which provides the title of Kaufman and Hart's *You Can't Take It With You,* a light comedy which was produced in 1936 and which won the Pulitzer Prize for Drama the next year, when *No Pockets in a Shroud* was published.

In addition to existentialism, there is also a strong element of conventional American naturalism running through McCoy's fiction. These philosophies are in some respects congruent, but in others contradictory. Both are essentially pessimistic, in that they posit an unfriendly cosmos. For the existentialist, however, it is possible to attain a certain stoic dignity through knowledge of one's world and of one's self. Although we are not free to alter our external circumstances to any great degree, we are free to determine our attitude toward those circumstances. If the substance of things is immutable, it is still possible to fall back on style.

In contrast, the naturalist sees free will as either non-existent or without great consequence. Characters in a naturalistic novel tend to be cogs in a mechanistic universe. Reduced to the level of higher animal life, they are not noted for metaphysical insight. The problem with Michael Dolan is that he is intended to be an existential hero, but never quite transcends the role of naturalistic victim. One feels that had he been accepted by the elite of Colton society, his career as a rebel probably would have been abandoned.

Like naturalists as diverse as Stephen Crane and Thomas Hardy, McCoy was obsessed with the very contingency of experience. A trivial action can set in motion an entire chain of events which leads to a seemingly unrelated catastrophe. Since it is impossible to foresee all of the ramifications of any given "choice," life itself is largely a matter of random circumstances. This point is made rather explicitly in the early pages of *No Pockets in a Shroud* and is repeated periodically throughout the novel.

When Myra first meets Dolan and discovers that he has quit his job, she says to Eddie Bishop: "If I had been one minute later getting out of bed this morning . . . , if I had stopped to get my usual cup of coffee . . . , I would have missed seeing you. And if I had missed being here Dolan undoubtedly would have gone and begged for his job back. And he would have gotten it, too. But now he won't" (pp. 10-11). As Michael proceeds to realize his destiny, the occurrences of that morning seem retrospectively more ominous. Finally, when he falls in the alley on the novel's last page, his dying thought is: "Suppose Myra *had* stopped that day for that cup of coffee?"

(p. 307).

Although *No Pockets in a Shroud* is set in a community which resembles Dallas, the Western locale is incidental to the novel's thematic content. McCoy's story would not have been appreciably different had it taken place in, say, the South or the Midwest. The same is not true of his next novel, *I Should Have Stayed Home* (1938). Published seven years after his arrival in Hollywood, *I Should Have Stayed Home* is typical of the Wasteland fiction which came out of Southern California in the 1930s. Indeed, one critic observed: "Horace McCoy hates Hollywood, not enough to stay away from it but enough to get all the bile out of his system in a short, bitter, name-calling novel" (*Saturday Review*, February 19, 1938, p. 4).

McCoy was simply one of many writers who migrated to Southern California in the 1930s. With the development of sound in motion pictures in the late twenties, there came an increasing need for movie dialogue. Accordingly, some of the finest writers of the twentieth century—William Faulkner, F. Scott Fitzgerald, Nathanael West, Aldous Huxley, Christopher Isherwood, James M. Cain, and Theodore Dreiser, to name only a few—moved west to supply that need at a considerably higher price than they could then command for their fiction. Referred to by Jack Warner as "schmucks with Underwoods" (see Tom Dardis, *Some Time in the Sun*, p. 8), many of these writers took offense at the tawdriness of Hollywood and felt themselves artistically compromised.

This land to which they had come had been identified throughout New World history with the quest for a western El Dorado. Indeed, ever since our first parents were exiled from paradise by being driven to the *east* of Eden, the attempt to recover primordial bliss has frequently involved a journey west. As the frontiers of the new Eden were pushed as far west as they could go, the hopes which were once vested in all of America came to rest exclusively in California.

And yet, the new Adam is no more capable than the old of returning to his original innocence. Rather than being barred by cherubim with flaming swords, his path simply comes to an end at the Pacific Coast. As Jonas Spatz writes: "The westward movement, once symbolic of rebirth out of Old World privilege, oppression, and poverty, becomes a journey into despair. The American is betrayed not by the brutalities of the city but by the image of his own salvation" (*Hollywood in Fiction: Some Versions of the American Myth*, p. 114).

The ambience of Southern California, and particularly that of Hollywood, can be seen as both the geographic and mythic culmination of our age-long quest for the Heavenly city, quite literally "the City of Angels." Consequently, this region is just as paradoxical as that quest itself. In addressing himself to this point, Spatz observes:

> Hollywood, as the western boundary of the frontier movement, is the land of abundance and growth, of sunshine and eternal spring. Its motion pictures recapture the optimism and moral certainty of a vanished age, and its movie stars symbolize a vanished innocence. . . . The vision of Hollywood is born of expectation and disappointment, external success and inner failure. (p. 116)

Such a vision permeates Horace McCoy's third novel.

The principal characters in *I Should Have Stayed Home*—two unemployed movie extras and platonic roommates, Ralph Carston and Mona Matthews—share a bungalow and wait in vain to become overnight screen stars or at least to get a call from Central Casting. An even more frustrated friend of theirs is apprehended shoplifting and later hangs herself in her cell.

The fortunes of Ralph and Mona improve when the couple is invited to a Hollywood party so decadent that it prefigures Claude Estee's bash in Nathanael West's *The Day of the Locust* (1939).

There, they rub shoulders with the great, the near-great, and the merely perverse. As a result, Mona becomes stand-in for a lesbian starlet and Ralph gigolo to a kinky senior citizen.

Although Mona makes it on to a movie lot, her career is aborted when her efforts at union organizing cause her to be fired. Ralph, however, progresses no farther than his sponsor's bed and is eventually replaced there by a young opportunist who is content to settle for money without fame. As the novel ends, Mona marries a rancher whom she meets through an advertisement in a lonelyhearts magazine and Ralph continues to dream of stardom.

Although he focuses on two poverty-stricken young people, McCoy broadens the social scope of his novel by introducing Ralph's wealthy admirer Mrs. Smithers. Ironically, these two are brought together as an indirect result of Mona's friendship with Sam Lally, the man with whom she had lived before meeting Ralph. Mona has won some local notoriety by being jailed for contempt when she insults the judge at the shoplifting trial of her friend Dorothy Trotter. Sam, who has gone on to become Mrs. Smithers' live-in lover, is dispatched to invite Mona to one of his employer's parties. When Mona insists that Ralph also be invited, she loses a second male companion to the old lady's predatory lust.

The party itself is a microcosm of upper-level Hollywood society. When Ralph is unable to conceal his embarrassment at the fact that a comely young actress is swimming in the nude, Lally tells him: "This is Hollywood, old man, . . . where morality never crosses the city limits" (p. 26). As it turns out, the gathering is actually a benefit for the Scottsboro Boys, a group of vagrant blacks who had been falsely accused of raping a white woman in Alabama and whose case became a *cause célèbre* for the American Left. Ralph, who is himself a native of Georgia, has never heard of the Scottsboro Boys; however, he comes close to making a scene at the party when he expresses outrage at the amorous behavior of an interracial couple.

One guest at the party, a screenwriter named Heinrich, is an eccentric who jumps into swimming pools fully clothed, who shows up at formal dinners in a sweatshirt, and who yells like Tarzan while hanging from trees. He is, according to James Agee, "one magnificently successful character" ("On the Bookshelf/'Are Hollywood Stars Sub-normal or Sub-human,'" *Table Talk*, July 14, 1938, p 16). Heinrich has learned that if one cannot make it in Hollywood on the basis of ability, it is nevertheless possible to establish a reputation with an offbeat personality. In a moment of candor, he tells Ralph:

> When I came out here, I was still a good reporter, but nobody would give me a job. . . . So I figured that this was a sucker town and that a smart guy could hit big. I started doing screwy things . . . , and you know what happened? I'll tell you. The studios fought for me. They thought I was a genius. So now I'm getting two grand a week. (p. 175)

Just prior to this revelation, Heinrich has entertained a group of Hollywood celebrities at Mrs. Smithers' dinner table. When his hostess asks him to come up with a story-idea for a film, he climbs on to the table, kicks some plates aside, and begins to improvise a tale about a young lady who is on the verge of setting a world's record for being buried alive.

With just twenty-four hours to go, this girl becomes sexually aroused by a man whose voice she hears through a speaking tube. Over the objections of her manager, she insists on being dug up so that she can meet the man behind the seductive voice. Although he is hideously ugly and knows that she will be repulsed the minute she sees him, this man allows the girl to be resurrected. As he explains to her manager: "This girl wants me to the exclusion of all other men in the world. . . . In the two or three hours they are digging her up, until the actual moment she sees me, I am the greatest lover in the world" (p. 174).

This story-idea, like the marathon-dance setting in *They Shoot Horses,* depicts one of the more macabre fads of the thirties. In a slightly altered form, Heinrich's tale was elaborated by McCoy into a 1945 short story called "The Girl in the Grave." Its author's only serious work of fiction in the ten years between *I Should Have Stayed Home* and *Kiss Tomorrow Good-bye,* this story "can be read as a complex psychological allegory of McCoy's internal agonizing over his own self-interment in Hollywood and denial of his artistic longings" (Sturak, p. 378).

· Although not as baldly autobiographical as *No Pockets in a Shroud, I Should Have Stayed Home* is also derived from its author's personal experiences and observations. Ralph Carston is a Little Theatre actor who, like McCoy, starred in the role of Joe in *They Knew What They Wanted.* Also, like McCoy, he is lured to Hollywood with the promise of a screentest.

Despite these similarities, however, it would be wrong to view Ralph as his creator's alter-ego. For one thing, Ralph's chances for success are precluded by the coming of talkies. After listening to his Southern accent, one producer says: "if this was in the days of silent pictures I'd have you a star within a week. But not now, not with sound" (p. 62). Of course, the advent of sound was the very thing which made it possible for McCoy and his fellow writers to have their time in the sun. In addition, Ralph is too irredeemably naive to be an accurate reflection of McCoy's own personality. At the end of the novel he seems no wiser than at the beginning.

Carston even fares badly when compared to his female counterpart. Consider, for example, their differing reactions to Dorothy Trotter's suicide. In one of the novel's most melodramatic scenes, Mona places several fan magazines in Dorothy's lifeless grasp and tells a pack of vulturous photographers who want a picture of the "instrument of death," that "that's what really killed her" (p. 162). Mona then gives up her own star-crossed ambitions by signing on as a stand-in and eventually leaves Hollywood altogether. Ralph, on the other hand, seems relatively unaffected by Dorothy's fate and simply redoubles his efforts to get a foot inside the door of a major studio.

One of the staples of the Hollywood novel is sexual perversion. In this reverse Eden, romantic love degenerates beyond normal physical lust into a frantic, onanistic search for gratification. For his own contribution to this genre, McCoy tells a fairly traditional tale, but one in which the conventional sex roles are reversed. Ralph, the (literally) virginal hero from rural America, comes to the wicked city where an insatiable older lover purchases his favors with material gifts and promises of fame.

A woman of decidedly sado-masochistic tendencies, Mrs. Smithers is old enough to be the boy's mother. "She grabbed my head between her hands again," Ralph tells us, "and kissed me furiously all over the face, biting my chin. I put my hands on her shoulders, not pushing her away this time, just holding her off. I could feel the wrinkles of skin between my fingers. It made me a little sick" (pp. 83-84).

If *No Pockets in a Shroud* suffers from having an implausibly superhuman protagonist, *I Should Have Stayed Home* falls prey to a nearly opposite pitfall — Ralph Carston is just too stupid to produce much reader empathy. Despite all of the things that happen to him, his personality remains essentially static. Perhaps this flatness of characterization represents a conscious effort on McCoy's part to dramatize the stultifying effects of life in Hollywood. If so, the author simply has succumbed to the fallacy of imitative form.

Philosophically, there is little existentialism in this novel — no code of heroic stoicism, no grace under pressure. The characters are acted upon by forces they scarcely understand and are powerless to control.

Toward the end of the novel, Mona says to Ralph: "You know what I think? I think your whole future is mapped out from the day you're born, from the day you're even conceived, and that no matter what you do, you can't beat it. There's no escape" (p. 211).

In many ways *Kiss Tomorrow Good-bye* is Horace McCoy's most amibitious work of fiction. Written after he had been away from serious artistic concerns for several years and at a time when his European reputation was at its height, this novel is an attempt to introduce Freudian insights into the framework of a *Black Mask* tale. According to Philip Durham, McCoy's "application of the objective technique to psychoanalytical problems has carried the technique to its furthest development" ("The Objective Treatment of the 'Hard-Boiled' Hero in American Fiction: A Study in the Frontier Background of Modern American Literature," Diss. Northwestern University 1949, p. 263).

The novel's protagonist is a psychopathic criminal who uses the aliases Ralph Cotter and Paul Murphy. As the story opens, he escapes from prison with the aid of a fellow-inmate's sister — the sexually promiscuous Holiday Tokawanda. Cotter-Murphy then resumes his former lifestyle by blackmailing the corrupt local police into abetting his future crimes.

The plot becomes more complicated when its protagonist visits a physician with established underworld connections. This physician has forsaken his medical practice, and — with the help of his assistant Margaret Dobson, the eccentric, spoiled daughter of a local tycoon — is now promoting a vague mystical creed. After Cotter-Murphy becomes romantically involved with Margaret and is tricked into marrying her, he has the opportunity to collect $35,000 from her father in exchange for an annulment. Unlike Michael Dolan, however, he balks at such a proposal. If he takes Ezra Dobson's money, the protagonist reasons, the old man might check out his background. He thinks it best to let sleeping bloodhounds lie.

While preparing to celebrate after the biggest heist of his career, Cotter-Murphy is summoned to the Dobson mansion. Ezra has been so impressed with "Paul's" character and with his salutary influence on Margaret that he is now willing to bribe the young man into letting the marriage stand. Although the practical benefits of such an arrangement are almost ideal, the protagonist is troubled by his subconscious association of Margaret with his own dead grandmother.

He leaves his prospective wife on the golf course of her country club and returns to his apartment, unarmed. During his absence, Holiday has discovered that it was actually Cotter-Murphy—not the police—who had killed her brother. As the novel closes, she gains revenge by gunning down the protagonist.

Although McCoy uses first-person point of view, the reader tends not to identify with the narrator of *Kiss Tomorrow Good-bye*. The access which we are afforded into his consciousness, by means of interior monologue, reveals a pathologically insecure person who uses sex and violence as modes of defense. Distasteful as he may be, however, Cotter-Murphy is—in many ways—a cut above the ordinary criminal.

To begin with, McCoy's protagonist possesses a considerable intellect. He is a college graduate with a Phi Beta Kappa key and a knowledge of Greek mythology. In addition, he has a fastidious sense of taste. When a cop with whom he is doing business enters his apartment chewing on a toothpick, Cotter-Murphy thinks: "This stupid, oestrual son-of-a-bitch" (p. 137), and offers the man some dental floss.

Later, in a delicatessen frequented by police, McCoy's protagonist experiences nausea witnessing the patrons' deplorable table manners:

They just sat there, talking and chewing and drinking; everybody in the place was talking and chewing and drinking, and in my mind I saw in every mouth what I had seen in the turnkey's mouth, a loathsome bolus: these swine, these offals, and I could not eat the sandwich. (p. 182)

Like Ralph Carston and like McCoy himself, Cotter-Murphy is a Southerner who has gone west (although the novel's setting is never specified, it is apparently a short bus ride from Arizona). Also, he shares his creator's fondness for the good things in life, even going so far as to send his cognac back at a restaurant when it proves to be the wrong brand. Moreover, when he sees her brother Jonah's wardrobe, the protagonist is almost persuaded to marry Margaret Dobson.

There can be little doubt that Cotter-Murphy thinks himself superior to the riffraff with whom he is forced to associate. Not only does he want them to concede his greater intelligence, he is also intent on their regarding him as at least their equal in toughness. Nothing provokes him to violent fits of rage as quickly as aspersions upon his hard-boiled image. When one of his cohorts accuses him of putting on an act, the protagonist viciously kicks that man's club foot. Much later, when a corrupt police inspector calls him a "swell-headed punk," Cotter-Murphy snarls: "I'm no goddamn dilettante playing around the edges of the underworld for a vicarious thrill; I'm just as much a professional as you are" (p. 264).

As J. Thomas Sturak points out, the prototype for Cotter-Murphy can be found in a character introduced in McCoy's last *Black Mask* story "Somebody Must Die" (October 1934). Here, the flying Texas Ranger Jerry Frost encounters a notorious smuggler at the latter's Mexican hideout. Like the protagonist of *Kiss Tomorrow Good-bye*, this smuggler—Nicholas Harmon—is a Phi Beta Kappa who has turned to a life of crime. Harmon is proud of his academic accomplishments, which include a masters degree from M.I.T., and appears unusually introspective for a *Black Mask* villain. Similarly, there is an element of intellectual snobbery in Cotter-Murphy. At one juncture in the novel, he makes a point of purchasing a Phi Beta Kappa key from a local pawn shop.

Of course, by 1948, the figure of the genius-criminal was familiar to gangster movie aficionados. What makes Cotter-Murphy more than just a stock character are the psychological quirks which motivate his behavior. Although the experience most crucial to the shaping of his personality is not revealed until the novel's final pages, it is clear from the outset that McCoy's protagonist is operating from deep-seated compulsions.

His violent reactions to skepticism concerning his toughness betray Cotter-Murphy's own self-doubts. In addition, he has a sensitive stomach which becomes excruciatingly painful whenever he experiences fear. At the emotional level, he is less a macho criminal than a bewildered child. He even seems, at times, to be striving for a return to infantile contentment. In one richly symbolic scene, the protagonist—just sprung from prison—curls up in an old station wagon with a box of Fig Newtons and two bottles of milk:

> This was wonderful, being hemmed up in the station wagon nice and cosy and in the half-dark that felt vaguely familiar, vaguely reminded me of something and I sipped the milk experimentally, for the first taste of something you have craved for a long time is never what you have imagined it will be, but after the fourth or fifth sip I knew that this was finally the real thing. (p. 33)

Long before the end of *Kiss Tomorrow Good-bye,* we suspect that Cotter-Murphy suffers from some kind of sexual neurosis. His ambivalent attitudes toward homosexuality are a case in point. Early in the novel, he is so offended by the erotic advances of a fellow prisoner that he murders the man while making his escape. Then, later on, he all but reverses his bias. When his business takes him to a "pansy joint," he discovers his affinity with its clientele. "They were rebels too," he tells us, "rebels introverted; I was a rebel extraverted—theirs was the force that did not kill, mine was the force that did kill" (p. 278). Although the catalyst for this change of heart is never made clear, the protagonist apparently realizes that his life—like that of the deviate—is shaped by sexual determinism.

On the surface, the concept of determinism would seem to contradict Cotter-Murphy's own explicit belief in free will. "I came into crime through choice and not through environment," he tells Holiday. "I need no apologist or crusader to finally hold my lifeless body up to the world and shout for them to come and observe what they have wrought" (p. 254). We must remember, however, that McCoy's protagonist is a dramatic character, not his creator's mouthpiece. (Determinism does not rule out the illusion of freedom, only its reality.) Moreover, the focus of Cotter-Murphy's speech is sociological; he says nothing about subconscious *psychic* drives.

The novel's protagonist is caught up in a familiar kind of romantic conflict. As Leslie Fiedler points out in *Love and Death in the American Novel*, one of the recurring situations in our fiction is that in which a single character (male or female) is torn between two very different kinds of lovers. When it is a man who faces such a dilemma, he frequently must choose between an ethereal maiden and a concupiscent earth-mother. Typically (as in *The Blithedale Romance* and *Pierre*), the former of these is fair and blonde, and the latter dark and brunette. The two women in Cotter-Murphy's life conform to a similar dichotomy, except that the color symbolism appears to be reversed. Although Holiday's hair color is never specified, the first thing that strikes the protagonist about Margaret is that "her hair was black, a livid black, my God, you never saw hair so black" (p. 110).

Holiday is a totally physical woman. Her sexual appetites are voracious and she satisfies them indiscriminately. She even inspires Cotter-Murphy to bursts of purple prose, as when he describes her unadorned body as "the Atlantis, the Route to Cathay, the Seven Cities of Cibola" (p. 25). These treasures, we learn, must be violently attacked to be fully enjoyed.

Margaret, on the other hand, is other-worldly. A devout believer in the cosmic mumbo-jumbo expounded by Doc Green, she seems to regard her sexual trysts with the protagonist in a detached, metaphysical light. And Cotter-Murphy apparently is of a similar mind. On the occasion of their first copulation, he tells her: "Don't move a muscle now. . . . Don't even breathe" (p. 160). He is perpetually fascinated by her and even drawn to her, but his "desire" for her seems to border on the necrophilic.

When the protagonist first encounters Margaret and compliments her on wearing *Huele de Noche* perfume, she replies that she is not wearing perfume. Later, he realizes that he had been thinking of the *Huele de Noche* bushes at his grandmother's funeral, because Margaret's complexion—rendered pale by its contrast with her black hair—had evoked the memory of his grandmother in her coffin. This impressionistic association plagues him throughout the remainder of the novel.

In the climactic scene on the country club golf course, Cotter-Murphy's stream-of-consciousness recollections finally clarify the childhood trauma which has made him what he is. As a young boy, he had lived with his grandparents, and whenever he was in danger of incurring his grandfather's wrath for having committed some mischief, he would hide underneath his grandmother's capacious skirt. This expedient worked well until, one day, he began exploring his grandmother's legs. Enraged, the old lady threatened to inform the boy's grandfather and predicted that the lad's punishment would be the same as had been recently inflicted on one of the family's rams—castration.

Panicked, the child sought to silence his grandmother by hitting her on the head with a rock. When the blow proved lethal, he pretended that she had fallen off a horse. Although he had suppressed the terrible truth of what had happened, merely being with Margaret brings it all back. Fearing that he might harm himself or others in what appears to her an inexplicable trance, Margaret takes the protagonist's gun away from him. Following this symbolic castration, he walks away from her, saying: "I killed you once. . . . Do not make me kill you again" (p. 366).

With the novel's psychological riddle fully explained, McCoy delivers Cotter-Murphy to his almost redundant death at Holiday's hands: "I could see nothing and I could feel nothing, but I had a vestige of awareness left that made me know that I was pulling my knees up and pushing my chin down to meet them, and that at last I was safe and secure in the blackness of the womb from which I had never emerged . . ." (p. 372; ellipsis in text).

If *Kiss Tomorrow Good-bye* is McCoy's most artistically venturesome novel, *Scalpel* is much the opposite. A conventional potboiler about a handsome and talented surgeon, this book made its author ten times more money—even before it was begun—"than all of his previous published fiction together" (Sturak, p. 518). Originally sold as a screen treatment to Hal Wallis Productions for a figure that has been estimated as being between $50,000 and $100,000, *Scalpel* remained on the *New York Times* "Best-Seller" list for nearly three months and eventually sold fifteen thousand copies. Although hardly a spectacular success when compared to the works of James A. Michener or Harold Robbins, Horace McCoy's fifth novel gave its creator his first taste of financial security.

Scalpel's protagonist, Dr. Thomas Owen, is a combination

Renaissance Man-Byronic Hero. Born and raised in a southern Pennsylvania coal town and educated at the University of Pennsylvania, Owen becomes a legendary Army surgeon who is decorated for bravery and who is given two pearl-handled revolvers by General Patton. Returning to civilian life, he establishes a lucrative practice and gains entrance to the upper levels of Pittsburgh society with the aid of an admiring coal heiress.

No matter how high he rises socially and economically, however, Owen is still a product of his birthplace—Coalville. Unfortunately, his family is hated there because the town blames a recent cave-in on the corrupt practices of Tom's brother Lloyd—a high-living mine inspector. As a result, their mother must be moved to Pittsburgh for her own safety. Nevertheless, she maintains a neurotic attachment to the old hometown.

Meanwhile, Tom's professional reputation has been enhanced by a couple of brilliant operations on wealthy patients. In the process, he falls in love with his scrub nurse Joan Lasher, who is herself engaged to one of Owen's younger colleagues. In the last half of the novel, Lasher helps Owen to realize his gift for healing and to lose some of his *nouveau-riche* cynicism. As a consequence of several dramatic plot developments, Tom decides—quite selflessly—to send his beloved back to her original fiancé and to give up private practice to teach surgery at Harvard. Still, he gains a kind of consolation prize by rewinning the hand of his socialite-sponsor—the jet set heiress Helen Curtis.

Scalpel is an extremely facile product which shows the effects of McCoy's two decades of screenwriting. Structurally, the novel divides into two sections of relatively equal length. Tom Owen's rise to social prominence and his relationship with Helen Curtis dominate the first half of the narrative, while his discovery of his vocation and his affair with Joan Lasher are the focus of the second half. In addition, the

Coalville subplot weaves itself throughout the entire novel.

We can find in this work many of the same conflicts which we see in McCoy's previous fiction; however, here they tend to be resolved in such a way as to leave everybody happier at the end of the novel than at its beginning. Like McCoy's other protagonists, Tom Owen is an outsider who strives for upward mobility. But, unlike those other protagonists, he actually achieves that mobility and a high degree of self-knowledge as well. Moreover, the women in his life make him stronger rather than weaker. In other words, *Scalpel* is largely a thematic inversion of McCoy's other four novels.

For one thing, Helen Curtis is a creation unique to the McCoy canon—a decent, mature, sophisticated, basically unselfish *rich* woman. Owen may be a peasant who has become a gentleman only "by act of Congress" (p. 22), but Helen is every inch a lady. At one point, Tom says of her: "She looked the way water cress tastes" (p. 83); and later, he toasts her as "the most attractive woman in the world who is also the only woman in the world who knows the difference between grammar and syntax" (p. 185).

If Helen is an unprecedented McCoy character, Owen clearly is not. As a projection of the author's own self-image, he is an even more fantastic creation than Michael Dolan. Perhaps sensing that he would never fully realize his own ambitions, McCoy achieved them vicariously through the figure of Tom Owen. To understand the scope of those ambitions, we need only turn to a letter which McCoy had written two decades before the publication of *Scalpel*. "Wouldn't it be swell when you're fifty," he imagined, "to know that you were a great director, a great actor, a great writer and a great musician or painter? . . . Who in history ever turned the trick? Cellini? . . . Casanova? . . . Michaelangelo? . . . Da Vinci? . . . Not quite" (see Sturak, p. 530).

Provided we can muster the requisite suspension of disbelief, Owen is an undeniably appealing character. He represents an almost perfect blend of primitive authenticity and aristocractic refinement. Demonstrating the former, he comments on a typical upper-class party:

> It used to be in the days when this country was tough and strong and was being built that a man went out and killed a bear and lugged it home for the neighbors' pleasure and that was a social triumph. Now that the building's over and the country is flat and flabby, the great-great-grandsons go out and trap a [homosexual] social columnist and lug him home to dinner and *that's* a social triumph. (p. 105)

Owen is also a college football hero, an incomparable lover, and a two-fisted drinker who seems never to suffer from a hangover. (Mr. Mitty, call your office.)

Although he may have been born to a coalmining family, Tom has done an admirable job of getting the dirt out from under his fingernails. He has a deep appreciation for the paintings of Utrillo; and when Helen expresses surprise at his casual mention of having known the man, Owen replies just as casually: "Yes, I know him. Picasso took me there once" (p. 159). He also reads obscure poems by Baudelaire and is something of an artist himself. As Lasher tells him: "Beautiful surgery contains as much emotion as beautiful music or beautiful poetry. You push it past the boundaries of science and make it an art" (p. 251).

The supreme irony of the first half of the novel is Owen's ignorance of his own surgical talent. He honestly believes himself to be a hack who needs to cultivate wealthy patients in order to establish a reputation. "The measure of a doctor's success," he tells Lasher, "is his clientele" (p. 240). Although Owen has performed remarkably well under the most adverse circumstances while in the Army, he dismisses these accomplishments on the grounds that wounded soldiers are dispensable in a way that prominent civilians are not.

Since the story is narrated from the protagonist's point of view, the reader does not realize for some time that Owen is in fact a medical genius. Our first hint that this may be the case comes when he attends a party in Pittsburgh and runs into a general on whom he had once operated. A noted local physician sitting at the same table says to Tom: "As the General's doctor, Colonel, my belated congratulations. . . . It was a beautiful operation" (p. 97). Then, further into the novel, Lasher tries to explain to Owen the effect which his war-time heroics have had on her fiancé. "Crowley came to serve because you are responsible for him being a surgeon," she says. "You showed him the light. . . . You are his God" (p. 178).

From his initial encounter with Lasher until the end of the novel, Tom gradually becomes convinced of his own ability in the operating room. As a result, he is the only character in any of McCoy's novels to experience genuine spiritual growth. Metaphysically, his characterization of Tom Owen may represent a great advance in the author's moral vision; however, between McCoy's intention and his actual accomplishment, he encountered serious difficulties in formulating a credible plot.

At his best, as in *They Shoot Horses, Don't They?* and *Kiss Tomorrow Good-bye*, McCoy depicts the reaction of individuals to external events. At his worst — and, with the possible exception of *No Pockets in a Shroud*, *Scalpel* surely is McCoy at his worst — he is content to orchestrate external events for the purpose of enhancing the fortunes of his protagonist. There is perhaps more truth than McCoy realized in Tom Owen's oft-repeated quip: "God was in His Heaven and all was right with the scriptwriter." In pondering the coincidences which seem to control Owen's life, we are apt to suspect that God and the scriptwriter (a.k.a. Horace McCoy) are one and the same. Moreover, should we fail to note these coincidences when they occur, we are given an explicit summary of them in a conversation which Tom has with Helen Curtis.

Had he not stopped for a train which he might have beaten across the tracks, Owen tells Helen, he probably would not have met her when he did. Then, months later, when the wealthiest woman in Pittsburgh becomes ill at a party and neither of her regular doctors can be reached, Tom is both available and uncharacteristically sober. (As the litany continues, we are reminded of Myra's failure to stop for her usual cup of coffee at the beginning of *No Pockets in a Shroud*.) "Now the dogmatists can call these things coincidences if they like," Tom concludes, "and I won't argue with them . . . , but from where I'm standing they seem to form some sort of pattern" (p. 299).

Tom Owen's progress toward self-knowledge is facilitated by three crucial operations, all of which are performed in the second half of the novel. The first of these involves Mrs. Henry Nelson, the Dowager-Empress of Pittsburgh society. Ironically, this operation — which he sees as being his ticket to fame and fortune — is the one which provokes his first confrontation with Lasher. She is appalled by his greed and cynicism and tries to convince him of the extent of his talent. At this point, however, all that he is willing to concede is that he is capable of excellent surgery as long as she is by his side.

After his next operation, Owen's confidence in himself grows considerably. On this occasion, he performs a complicated surgical procedure flawlessly, in record time, and without Lasher's assistance (to rid him of his dependence on her, she has ducked out at the last moment). Finally, when another cave-in occurs at Coalville, he faces great risk by going down into a dangerous section of the mine to perform a life-saving leg amputation. Not only has he come to appreciate his own brilliance as a surgeon, but he also has achieved psychological independence, has become reconciled with his past, and has begun to recognize his responsibility to serve mankind.

McCoy never makes it sufficiently clear why, in the aftermath of these formative experiences, Owen urges Lasher to return to Crowley. To be sure, she has accomplished her utilitarian function—"it was as if Lasher herself was a scalpel cutting through all the artificialities I had acquired, all the hatreds I had built and the fears I had inherited from God only knows how far back" (p. 296)—but it scarcely seems credible that Tom would so easily give up the woman he loves. Indeed, since he has decided to teach at Harvard, his new circumstances would appear to be ideal for a wife who wanted to study surgery. If he has discovered that it was not love—but temporary need—which drew him to her, he gives no indication that that is the case.

The ending of *Scalpel* resembles nothing so much as the ending of *Casablanca*. In McCoy's version, Lasher is the passionate heroine who is persuaded to devote her life to inspiring an idealist whom she does not love. And Owen is the tough-talking, but infinitely noble, hero who gives her up. When last we see him, he is joining forces with an old pal who—unlike Claude Rains—is rich, seductive, and female. It could well be the start of a beautiful friendship.

In striking contrast to *Scalpel, They Shoot Horses, Don't They?* is undoubtedly Horace McCoy's greatest and most famous novel. Never again was he able to achieve the tone of authenticity and the power of the metaphor which pervade this minor masterpiece. Like so many brilliant first novels, it was a promise never redeemed. Since its author will finally be remembered—if at all— for this one work, it is appropriate that a detailed discussion of *They Shoot Horses* conclude a study of Horace McCoy.

The story that McCoy tells is of the plight of a couple of struggling, Depression-era young people—Robert Syverton and Gloria Beatty. Both characters have been frustrated in their attempts to break into the movies. In desperation, they enter a marathon dance contest in which the dancers are required to keep moving for periods of an hour and fifty minutes, after which they enjoy ten minutes rest. The brutal spectacle continues for weeks as more and more of the original couples drop from fatigue. Indeed, the promoters of the marathon speed up the attrition rate by instituting derby races in which the contestants sprint around a painted track for fifteen minutes. Each night, the last couple to finish is eliminated from the dance.

From its inception the dance is attacked by a group of professional do-gooders—the Mother's League for Good Morals. The League's campaign against the marathon is so intense that the dance is forced to close after a shooting occurs in the adjoining beer garden. Embittered by life in general, Gloria walks out to the waterfront, removes a gun from her purse, and urges Robert to put her out of her misery. Responding with pity and in friendship, he complies. Our first and last glimpses of Robert come when he is standing in court, being sentenced for the murder of Gloria. The novel's title is derived from his poignant but ineffectual defense: "They shoot horses, don't they?"

What little critical attention this novel has received has tended to focus on its existentialist overtones. For example, Lee J. Richmond argues that "With the exception of Nathanael West's *Miss Lonelyhearts* and *The Day of the Locust*, McCoy's novel is indisputably the best example of absurdist existentialism in American fiction" ("A Time to Mourn and a Time to Dance: Horace McCoy's *They Shoot Horses, Don't They?*," *Twentieth Century Literature*, 17 [April 1971], 91). Also, it is clear that McCoy relished his reputation among continental intellectuals and probably altered the style of his last two novels in order to fit the role assigned to him as "the first American existentialist" (see Sturak, p. 400).

It is just as clear, however, that McCoy was not a conscious philosopher in the mold of Sartre and Camus. Instead, he was an artist who imaginatively anticipated many of the perceptions which would later become central to the existentialist world-view. Thus, existentialism can provide a useful, but limited, perspective from which to examine *They Shoot Horses, Don't They?*. Indeed, the very limitations of an existentialist critique bring into focus the critical problems which must be solved if we are to attain a full understanding of McCoy's novel.

The dance marathon is obviously meant to be more than just a grisly reminder of the historical period in which this story transpires. McCoy clearly did not intend to write a mere period-piece. In fact, we find that in the finished version of the novel, he has eliminated a number of the socio-economic allusions which appeared in an earlier short story on which the novel was based.

For example, in the short story, when Robert first meets Gloria, he asks her whether she wants to go to a movie or sit in the park. When she indicates that she would prefer the latter, he tells us that he is glad, "because I could live for three or four days on what two movie tickets cost" ("They Shoot Horses, Don't They," in *The Fourth Round: Stories for Men*, p. 305). In the novel, we find no reference to the cost of movie tickets, only the assertion that "it was always nice in the park" (p. 21).

A bit later in the short story, Gloria learns of Robert's ambition to become a movie director. When she asks him what kind of pictures he would make, he tells her, "Pictures about people like us. People who live in dark little rooms and work in factories" (p. 307). And when he decides to enter the marathon, Robert leaves his few possessions and extra clothing with his landlady: "until I could pay her all I owed her," he says. "She wasn't happy about it, but what else could she do?" (p. 307). The novel, however, contains neither the exchange with Gloria nor the reference to Robert's landlady.

Since *They Shoot Horses*—in its various revisions—became less identifiably the product of a particular historical situation, McCoy apparently wished to address himself to a universal human condition. The dance marathon is a sort of organic metaphor which movingly depicts the folly of all human endeavor when measured against the inexorable forces of time and mutability. Perhaps it is this symbolic dimension of the marathon which prompted Harry Levin to say: "If, as Camus . . . suggests, the human condition is that of Sisyphus, going through his motions eternally and ineffectually, it is easy to understand French admiration for . . . Horace McCoy's *They Shoot Horses, Don't They?*" ("Some European Views of Contemporary American Literature," *American Quarterly*, I [Fall 1949], 275).

In the midst of such eternal and ineffectual repetitions, it is impossible to find solace in traditional forms of meaning. Incapable of altering the circumstances of his life, the existential victim can nevertheless act purposefully by courting the annihilation of that life. For this reason, the significance of death is a primary concern of existentialism. The heroic existentialist believes that one knows the value of life only by risking death; while those who have despaired of finding meaning anywhere in life see suicide as the ultimate act of freedom. The Hemingway code hero falls into the former category; Gloria Beatty (and perhaps Hemingway himself) into the latter.

Unlike Nathanael West's Faye Greener, Gloria is too defeated and cynical to be a Hollywood coquette. Instead, she articulates an explicitly perverse view of romance and sexuality. During her first encounter with Robert, Gloria remarks: "I don't know whether the men stars can help me as much as the women stars. From what I've seen lately I've about made up my mind that I've been letting the wrong sex try to make me" (p. 22). Later in the same conversation, she describes her former liaison with a Syrian hot dog vendor:

"He chewed tobacco all the time . . . Have you ever been in bed with a man who chewed tobacco?" [ellipsis in text]

. . . . . .

"I guess I might even have stood that," she said, "but when he wanted to make me between customers, on the kitchen table, I gave up. A couple of nights later I took poison." (pp. 22-23)

In the midst of the marathon, however, Gloria is not above spending her ten-minute rest periods copulating with the master of ceremonies under the bandstand.

For Gloria, economic considerations take precedence over humanistic ones. Just as she entertains a relatively debased view of sexuality, so too does she see fertility as a curse rather than a blessing. Early in the novel, she advises a pregnant dance contestant to have an abortion. "What's the sense of having a baby," Gloria says, "unless you got dough enough to take care of it?" (p. 29). Although one might argue that Gloria is simply being realistic, she seems to raise the death-wish to the level of a metaphysical principle.

As is the case with normal sexuality, religious faith is also among those traditional forms of meaning which have been corrupted in the meretricious ambience depicted in the Hollywood novel. Such a corruption is evident in the tawdry funeral rituals of Evelyn Waugh's *The Loved One* and in the proliferation of exotic cults described in West's *The Day of the Locust*. But few displays of bogus religiosity can compare with the marriage of Vee Lovell and Mary Hawley in *They Shoot Horses, Don't They?*.

Far from being whimsical matchmakers, the promoters of the marathon are hard-headed businessmen. When one of them approaches Robert and Gloria with the idea of a public wedding, he says: "you can get divorced if you want to. It don't have to be permanent. It's just a showmanship angle" (p. 77). Although Gloria balks at the plan, Couple 71 (Vee and Mary) are persuaded to go along with it. And so a wedding takes place—complete with flowers, ushers, bridesmaids, and a minister named Oscar Gilder. In the chaotic, inverted world of McCoy's novel, it is ironically fitting that the Reverend Gilder's benediction be the twenty-third Psalm.

Curiously enough, Gloria is no atheist; however, the God in whom she believes is no benevolent deity. Instead, He is the force responsible for the world's being the way it is. About midway through the novel, Gloria says: "I wish God would strike me dead" (p. 76); and when she entreats Robert to shoot her, she tells him to "pinch-hit for God" (p. 127). Here, one is reminded of Gloucester's declaration in *King Lear*: "As flies to wanton boys, are we to th' gods, / They kill us for their sport."

Albert Camus once characterized suicide as being the "one truly serious philosophical problem." For him, "judging whether life is or is not worth living amounts to answering the fundamental question of philosophy" (*The Myth of Sisyphus*, p. 11). When Gloria answers that question in the negative, her decision is a conscious response to the Sisyphean dance of life. And her plight can be adequately understood in existentialist terms.

The case of Robert, however, raises some difficulties. At the beginning of McCoy's novel, Robert is down-and-out but optimistic. He does not share Gloria's nihilistic view of life and it is difficult to find a point in the novel when he consciously adopts her philosophy of defeat. And yet, by killing Gloria he is also turning himself over to the state for execution. To contemplate why Robert does so is to address oneself to a primary critical issue of this novel.

In McCoy's earlier short story, Gloria says to Robert: "Look—you've wanted to kill yourself, you've admitted it. You're just like I am, you haven't got the nerve. All right, you kill me and then the law'll kill you and neither one of us'll kill ourselves" (p. 312). By excluding this passage from the finished version of his novel, McCoy reduces Robert's consciousness of his fate. It seems to me that his virtual suicide is less a deliberate statement about the futility of life than an impulsive response to physical, mental, and even spiritual fatigue. Robert is a rather conventional fellow whose behavior is conditioned largely by external forces. To view his situation in any other light is to see his act of self-destruction as merely gratuitous.

There is another variation between the short story and novelistic versions of *They Shoot Horses* which I think bears on the question of Robert's consciousness. In the short story, Robert observes: "I think that's a lot of applesauce about people changing their destinies. You're put in a rut when you're born and you never get out of it. It's just like a fish. A fish is a fish when he is born and a fish when he dies. He can't make himself into an octopus by thinking hard, can he?" (p. 312). Such a declaration, complete with biological imagery, is clearly naturalistic in implication; however, it is somewhat anomalous for Robert to see his own condition quite so clearly. In a sense, the circumstances of McCoy's novel verify the determinism which his short story more baldly articulates. But in the novel, we do not encounter the contradiction of a character who *decides* that his fate is determined.

Though never explicitly discussed, the pall of determinism hangs very heavily over *They Shoot Horses*. The very structure of the novel sacrifices suspense for inevitability. We are apprised of the plot's climax on the first page of the text. What follows is largely explication and elaboration. Also, by rendering the judge's sentence in tabloid print—line-by-line, between each chapter, and increasing incrementally in point size—McCoy underscores the impersonal immensity of those leviathan-like forces which have overwhelmed Robert. Although he is not a victim exclusively of "society," Robert is destroyed by powers just as intractable as those which pronounce legal judgment upon him.

By choosing to tell his story from Robert's point of view, rather than from Gloria's, McCoy has deprived us of access to Gloria's consciousness. To a great extent, her function in the novel is determined by her actions toward Robert. Her attitude toward life and death, then, is simply the most important of many factors which influence her partner's fate. If Gloria can be viewed as a hard-core existential victim, Robert is just a naive country boy who has come to Hollywood in pursuit of the American Dream.

And it is precisely in this lack of singularity that Robert differs most from an existential figure. The striking surface parallels between Robert's perceptions in court and those of Camus' Meursault (see Sturak, pp. 405-07) serve only to accentuate the crucial difference between these two characters. Meursault is tried less for murder than for eccentricity. Robert, however, is an ordinary individual who finds himself capable of an extraordinary action. In this respect, his situation is quite similar to that of the typical naturalistic protagonist. As Donald Pizer points out, naturalism is "an extension of realism . . . in the sense that both modes often deal with the local and contemporary"; however, the naturalist discovers in the commonplace "the extraordinary and excessive in human nature" (*Realism and Naturalism in Nineteenth-Century American Literature*, p. 13).

In addition to his economic plight, one of Robert's greatest misfortunes is his inability to maintain any life-giving contact with the natural world. As a boy he had lived in pastoral surroundings on his grandfather's farm in Arkansas. Now he is confined, seemingly in perpetuity, to a dance-hall which epitomizes the worst excesses of a commercial, urban civilization. And yet, he compulsively searches out whatever sunlight becomes visible in that dance-hall, at one point even losing himself in a beautiful sunset.

Later he recalls:

> I lay there, thinking about the sunset, trying to remember what color it was. . . .
> Through the legs of my cot I could feel the ocean quivering against the piling below. It rose and fell, rose and fell, went out and came back, went out and came back. . . . [this second ellipsis is in the text]
> I was glad when the siren blew, waking us up, calling us back to the floor. (p. 51)

The sun can be seen as a symbol of time, the ocean of eternity. However, in the world of the dance marathon, time and eternity are hideously and frighteningly fused. Days and nights seem meaningless as time is measured in terms of "hours elapsed"; and the endlessness of time means only the endlessness of futile suffering.

Robert Syverton ultimately is done in by an accidental conjunction of circumstances. Although it may appear simplistic to say that he probably would have behaved differently had he had a good night's sleep, a square meal, and the promise of a job, no other explanation is nearly so consistent with the facts of the novel. It is the unconsciously victimized Robert, not the deliberately self-destructive Gloria, whose misery—like a dumb beast's—is terminated before he can realize its full horror. If suicide poses a philosophical problem, then it is one which sometimes is resolved for us.

Throughout the world, millions of people who would not recognize the name of Horace McCoy nevertheless have seen Sydney Pollack's 1969 motion picture version of *They Shoot Horses, Don't They?*. According to Pollack, there had been talk for many years of filming McCoy's novel—"it's said that one of the first to express interest was Charlie Chaplin" ("Forward to the Screenplay, " *They Shoot Horses, Don't They?*, p. 133)—but the down-beat mood of the story and its anti-Hollywood theme prevented the project from being realized until nearly three-and-a-half decades after the novel's publication.

On balance, Pollack's film is faithful to the spirit—if not the letter—of McCoy's novel. In addition to developing certain minor characters more fully, Pollack makes two fundamental changes in translating this story from print to celluloid. For one thing, he casts the marathon itself in time-present and depicts Robert's courtroom appearance with the flash-forward technique. "It seemed very important to the film," Pollack writes, "to create a sense of immediacy in the marathon itself" (p. 134). Furthermore, he has Robert and Gloria drop out of the dance before it is completed.

With the first of these major changes, Pollack loses as much in clarity as he gains in immediacy. The flash-forward sequences are distracting and confusing, especially since Pollack also uses flashbacks to Robert's childhood on his grandfather's farm. Indeed, the most prominent of these flashbacks—one in which a crippled horse is shot—may be superfluous as well as intrusive. As Paul Warshow points out:

> The sentence "They shoot horses, don't they?," both as the title and as Robert's final remark, is powerful enough in itself . . . and this scene merely weakens it, not just by being redundant, but by calling attention to the specific shooting of a specific horse and away from the idea which really gives the sentence its power: that there may be justice in putting any suffering animal (including a human being) out of its misery. ("The Unreal McCoy," in *The Modern American Novel and the Movies,* p. 35)

Although this incident is also redundant and thematically attenuating when it appears in the novel, McCoy at least makes the slain animal an old work horse rather than the beautiful stallion of Pollack's film.

The second major change which the movie makes in McCoy's story is far more effective. Pollack correctly criticizes the beer-garden shooting which ends the dance in the novel as being both arbitrary and needlessly melodramatic. It also raises the question of "what might have become of Gloria if the dance had played itself out" (Pollack, p. 135). In the film, the dance promoter tells Gloria that the only way she can make any money from the marathon is by agreeing to a public wedding with Robert. Even if she and Robert win first prize, their "expenses" will be deducted, leaving them a mere pittance. Upon making this discovery, the two partners drop out of the dance.

In the film, then, Gloria's death occurs against the backdrop of the *continuing* dance. The picture ends, immediately after Robert's climactic title line, with one final image of the marathon. We see "a long view of the dancers filing back onto the floor and beginning their excruciating parade all over again. . . . As the sign on top of the clock says, 'How long can they last?'" (Pollack, p. 135).

In effect, Pollack and his screenwriters Robert E. Thompson and James Poe have maintained greater metaphorical consistency than McCoy in their treatment of the dance marathon. As Warshow notes: "the marathon is a metaphor almost a priori: one of those natural . . . metaphors which grow out of the common core of our experience" (pp. 30-31). It is the inherent allegorical resonances of the marathon which make *They Shoot Horses* memorable as both novel and film. In none of his later works was McCoy able to find a controlling symbol nearly so powerful.

Any final assessment of Horace McCoy's contributions to literature must account for certain anomalies in his career. Probably the greatest of these is the disparity between his fame abroad and his obscurity at home. Although he was never an expatriate nor a particularly cosmopolitan writer, his popularity overseas has outlived him. In January 1966, over a decade after his death, a critical article celebrating the publication of the thousandth volume of the French *Serie Noire* listed McCoy—from among a group of 350 writers—as one of the series' ten "Grand Auteurs" (see Sturak, p. 409). And in a 1977 news broadcast, Harry Reasoner mentioned *They Shoot Horses, Don't They?* as one of the most popular movies in the People's Republic of China.

Of course, there is ample precedent for American writers being "discovered" in other countries prior to becoming acknowledged in the United States (Poe and Faulkner are two examples which immediately come to mind). It may be that the violent and decadent image of American life which one finds in McCoy's novels confirms what some foreign intellectuals want to believe. Also, the stylistic crudities which American critics have been quick to censure may be regarded in European eyes as part of McCoy's primitive charm. What remains to be seen is whether the makers of the American literary canon will—at long last—find room for a hitherto neglected native son.

If that native son's critical stock does rise, it probably will not be because of anything that has gone on in Paris or Peking. One finds McCoy's name mentioned most often not in treatises on existentialist or Marxist fiction, but in regionalist studies of the Hollywood novel. For this reason, we can say that—in addition to whatever else he may have been—Horace McCoy was a *Western* writer.

To clarify his position in Western American literature, however, it is necessary to distinguish among three types of regionalism. At the most superficial level, McCoy was a Westerner because he spent almost his entire adult life in Texas and California. More significantly, four of his five novels are set in the West. Beyond these considerations, though, is the fact that McCoy helped to define the literary image of Hollywood—a town which epitomizes one aspect of the Western myth.

In the work of Great Plains writers as diverse as Willa Cather, Frederick Manfred, and Wright Morris, we may well detect a sense of nostalgia and a dislike of modernity; but there is also a feel for the land which lends an elegiac note to their fiction. This is also true of John Steinbeck and Joan Didion when they are remembering their native Northern California. However, for those to whom the West means Southern California—and particularly Hollywood—the idea of the frontier is not so much a noble dream whose time has passed as it is a dangerous fraud whose perpetuity is not unlike that of a dance marathon. "When I am in California," wrote Theodore Roosevelt, "I am not in the West. I am west of the West." For Horace McCoy, California was indeed west of the West.

In recent years, revisionists like Tom Dardis, John Gregory Dunne, and Joan Didion (in her essays, though certainly not in her quintessentially nihilistic novel *Play It as It Lays*) have challenged the image of "Hollywood the Destroyer." Nevertheless, that image—whether accurate or not—seems to be a fixed part of our literary mythology. Although he may not have cut so tragic a figure as F. Scott Fitzgerald or Nathanael West, McCoy did his part to malign the town that he and his fellow "schmucks with Underwoods" loved to hate. Summing up their shared bitterness, the author of *The Great Gatsby* inscribed the following words in a friend's copy of that novel:

> From Scott Fitzgerald
> (Of doom a herald)
> For Horace McCoy
> (No harbinger of joy).

Selected Bibliography

Primary Sources
I Should Have Stayed Home. New York: Alfred A. Knopf, 1938.
Kiss Tomorrow Good-bye. New York: Random House, 1948.
No Pockets in a Shroud. London: Arthur Barker, 1937.
Scalpel. New York: Appleton-Century-Crofts, 1952.
They Shoot Horses, Don't They?. New York: Avon, 1969.
"They Shoot Horses, Don't They?." in *The Fourth Round: Stories for Men.* Edited by Charles Grayson. New York: Holt, 1953, pp. 304-313

Annotated List of Selected Criticism
Kael, Pauline. *Deeper Into Movies.* Boston: Little, Brown, 1973, pp. 68-72. In this mixed review, Kael finds Pollack's film of *They Shoot Horses* inferior to McCoy's original novel.
Pollack, Sydney. "Foreword to the Screenplay," in *They Shoot Horses, Don't They?* New York: Avon, 1969. This single paperback contains the text of botn the novel and the screenplay, as well as Pollack's informative discussion of the difference between the two.
Richmond, Lee J. "A Time to Mourn and a Time to Dance: Horace McCoy's *They Shoot Horses, Don't They?.*" *Twentieth Century Literature,* 17 (April 1971), 91-99. Richmond focuses on McCoy's incipient existentialism.
Sturak, J.Thomas. "Horace McCoy's Objective Lyricism," in *Tough Guy Writers of the Nineteen Thirties.* Edited by David Madden. Carbondale: Southern Illinois University Press, 1968, pp. 137-162. Sturak discusses McCoy's five novels, particularly *They Shoot Horses,* within the context of hard-boiled (*Black Mask* genre) fiction.
_____. "The Life and Writings of Horace McCoy, 1897-1955." Diss. UCLA 1967. Available through University Microfilms, this comprehensive and readable study is indispensable to serious McCoy scholarship.
Warshow, Paul. "The Unreal McCoy," in *The Modern American Novel and the Movies.* Edited by Gerald Peary and Roger Shatzkin. New York: Frederick Ungar, 1978, pp. 29-39. Despite certain reservations, Warshow regards the movie of *They Shoot Horses* as an improvement over the novel.

Wells, Walter. *Tycoons and Locusts*. Carbondale: Southern Illinois University Press, 1973, pp. 14-35. Within a single chapter, Wells discusses *They Shoot Horses* and James M. Cain's *The Postman Always Rings Twice* as examples of "Hollywood-Southland" fiction of the 1930s.

Other Works Cited

Agree, James. "On the Bookshelf/'Are Hollywood Stars Sub-normal or Sub-human.'" *Table Talk*, July 14, 1938, p. 16.

Borneman, Ernest. "Black Mask." *Go*, February-March 1952, pp. 63-66.

Camus, Albert. *The Myth of Sisyphus*. Translated by Justin O'Brien. London: Hamish Hamilton, 1955.

Dardis, Tom *Some Time in the Sun*. New York: Scribner's, 1976.

Durham, Philip. "The Objective Treatment of the 'Hard-Boiled' Hero in American Fiction: A Study in the Frontier Background of Modern American Literature," Diss. Northwestern University, 1949.

Killinger, John. *Hemingway and the Dead Gods: A Study in Existentialism*. Lexington: University of Kentucky Press, 1960.

Levin, Harry. "Some European Views of Contemporary American Literature." *American Quarterly*, 1 (Fall 1949), 264-279.

Pizer, Donald. *Realism and Naturalism in Nineteenth-Century American Literature*. Carbondale: Southern Illinois University Press, 1966.

Review of *I Should Have Stayed Home*. *Saturday Review*, February 19, 1938, p. 4.

Spatz, Jonas. *Hollywood in Fiction: Some Versions of the American Myth*. The Hague: Mouton, 1969.

Talmey, Allene. "Paris Quick Notes/About Sartre, Gide, Cocteau, Politics,/The Theatre, and Inflation." *Vogue*, January 15, 1947, p. 92.

A000030126063

813.54 Winch
Winchell, Mark Royden, 1948-

Horace McCoy /

Oregon State Library
Salem, 97310